TRUST ME

TRUST ME

by

WILLIAM J. MORIN

A HARVEST/HBJ BOOK
HARCOURT BRACE JOVANOVICH, PUBLISHERS
SAN DIEGO   NEW YORK   LONDON

Requests for permission to make copies of any part of the work
should be mailed to: Permissions Department,
Harcourt Brace Jovanovich, Publishers, 8th Floor,
Orlando, Florida 32887.

Library of Congress Catalog Number: 89-92534

ISBN 0-15-691350-X
Printed in the United States of America

First Harvest/HBJ Edition 1992

B C D E

To Mark, Timothy, and Jason Morin,
who have been—and continue to be—
the joy of my life.

To the employees of Drake Beam Morin,
who provide me daily inspiration.

ACKNOWLEDGMENTS

Credit must be given to Tim Lynch, who really put this book together. Tim is an outstanding writer and has collaborated with me on many projects in the past.

Special acknowledgment to Jo David, who, in the early days of the effort, gave invaluable assistance. Kudos to Eric Pomerance for transcribing raw thought into real words. Many thanks to Maureen Sullivan, my very able assistant and friend, without whose assistance this book never had a chance. Particular recognition to Dr. Elaine Duffy, who worked with me to develop the instruments herein that provide a measurement of trust between subordinates and management. And to Julie Bertini, whose diligent efforts have brought this book to press.

Finally, my special thanks must be reserved for the wonderful people at Drake Beam Morin, with whom I strive to establish a solid degree of non-dependent trust.

CONTENTS

Acknowledgments *vii*

Preface *xi*

1 "The Check Is in the Mail" *1*

2 Cradle to Grave *11*

3 New Rules and Old Loyalty *19*

4 The New Corporate Loyalty *27*

5 Non-Dependent Trust *41*

6 A Manager's Guide to Non-Dependent Trust *49*

7 Creating the Trust Environment *63*

8 The Language of Trust *73*

9 What's *Your* Trust Level? *85*

Afterword *101*

PREFACE

MY GRANDFATHER was a farmer in Kankakee, Illinois, where my father worked for the New York Central Railroad. My dad lost his job during the Depression, and he, my mother, sister, and two brothers moved back to the family farm.

My father never got over being terminated. He went back to work for the railroad two years later, and he stayed on the job until he retired, working the three-to-eleven shift, plus overtime, for thirty-five years. I don't think he ever missed a day. And I don't think there was ever a day when he wasn't concerned about his job.

He never recovered the ability to trust his superiors, or his company, or the free-enterprise system. He told us he felt locked in, afraid that his job would be taken away again. He's in his eighties now, and he still talks about the Depression, and about how debilitating it was to be out of work. Many people of his generation still dwell on those years.

My two brothers went to work as soon as they graduated from high school: Paul for a utility and Earl for a chemical company. Both became active in their unions, both were offered and accepted promotions into first-line management, and both lost those jobs. No longer protected by union contracts, but lacking the management skills or education that would allow them to move up from the bottom rungs of the management ladder, they were among the first to be fired when cutbacks were announced.

Both brothers found first-line supervisory jobs again, and kept them through their careers, but neither regained his faith in the system. Like my father, they were always concerned about job security. They had thought their companies would take care of them, that they would always have jobs if they worked hard and played "team ball."

I finished college, taught school for several years, and then went to work for a major consumer-products corporation. I took the job, in part, because I had been told that a huge computer at corporate headquarters tracked job openings throughout the organization. Once I joined the company, my skills and experience would be entered into the machine and updated at regular intervals. Then, whenever a position became open whose requirements matched my background, I would be considered for the new job.

That seemed like a fine system, and I certainly trusted that it would work for me. Several years—and several promotions—later, I was assigned to company headquarters. One of my first requests was to be shown the computer.

"There's never been such a thing," I was told.

I haven't forgotten my shattered feelings.

Recently, the son of a friend of mine graduated from college and took a job with a large advertising agency in New York. In the short time he's been with his company, he's seen one superior take credit for work *he* had done. Another supervisor remarked about a second assignment, "This is excellent work. *You* couldn't possibly have done it so quickly."

My friend's son asked me, "How did you put up with things like that?"

I told him, "It wasn't easy, it's just the way things were."

Today I am chairman and chief executive officer of Drake Beam Morin, Inc., which is generally considered the nation's leading human resources management consulting firm. I work with the top executives of many of the nation's largest corporations, advising them in employee relations, personnel management, and organizational change. I also work each year with thousands of American managers who went to work, did their jobs, and, for one reason or another, got fired. Virtually all these individuals are capable managers who've spent their time in the trenches and are anything but naive. But, one after another, I've heard their lament: "I trusted them, and look what they did to me."

These are eighties managers, who have seen industry after industry fall victim to offshore competition, or a falling dollar, or a rising dollar, or a Black Monday, or a management that fell asleep at the competitive switch.

If my experience—both in my work and within my own family—is any indication, we live in a world in which people genuinely want and need a sense of trust in their jobs and their companies. They aren't getting it.

That's what this book is about, trust and business. What does trust mean in the marketplace today? What should employees expect from their superiors and their companies? What can those companies afford to provide?

I believe American business has trapped itself in the inflated promises it has made. We've erected huge, tottering organizational skyscrapers in which employees feel a false security: "If I do my job, support the team, and keep my head down, there'll always be a job for me here."

But then competitive events shake the building, and management's hand is forced. Costs, overhead, and staff are cut, and a new group of disbelieving employees wonder why they trusted the company in the first place.

I think we've been living with a false sense of trust, the notion that job security can be divorced from individual and collective performance, that there is some additional, unwritten line beneath the bottom line that states, "You have a right to this job."

Trust Me addresses the challenge of restoring a new kind of trust to the workplace, a trust based on open, realistic communication rather than perceived rights and brokered privileges. I'm convinced that this form of trust can help companies and employees restore productivity and a competitive spirit in the marketplace.

Trust me!

1

"THE CHECK IS IN THE MAIL"

Debtor to lender: "The check is in the mail. Trust me."

Investor to CEO: "If I buy your company I won't change a thing. Trust me."

Male adolescent to female adolescent: "Trust me."

THE PHRASE is likely to be reserved for punch lines to old jokes today, but the implications are clear: trust is a risky business, a dangerous proposition. If patriotism is the last refuge of a scoundrel, trust may seem like the last asylum for a fool. When they hear the words "Trust me," wise men and wise women watch their backs.

Here's how one American businessman—myself—fell victim to his own misplaced sense of trust.

Early in my career, when I was sales manager for a manufacturing company, my superiors ordered me to reduce my sales staff by fifty people. I was a loyal company man: I'd been given an assignment and I headed out into the field to do my company's bidding.

I met my first victim in an airport motel room. He was happy to see me. "Bill, here's the dollar I owe you," he said.

"Keep it," I told him. "You're going to need it. You're fired."

The man fell back onto a bed, and for a moment I thought he was having a heart attack. I calmed him down and drove him home in his company car.

He told his wife and children. They were shocked and frantic at first, and then tearful. I collected his company credit cards, left the family with a severance check for about a month's salary, and drove away in his company car.

I still think about how ill-prepared and insensitive I had been that day. I still wonder if those children ever trusted a company again or had faith in the security of their father's job.

But I had a job to do, and, with practice, I got better at it and became, I think, more humane in the process. Fifty firings later, I reported back to the home office.

My boss called me into his office on that first day back from the field. "We've been getting a lot of phone calls," he said. "There's a real morale problem out there now, and I'm afraid we're going to have to let you go."

It was my turn to be shocked, so shocked that I didn't state the obvious: the company that ordered those terminations might have anticipated a morale problem. Later I learned that my termination had been planned all along. I had trusted my superiors, and look what they did to me. My salesmen had trusted me, and look what I did to them.

It took months to get over the sense of depression and loss I felt that day. I've never forgotten the feeling of being out of control, of being unable to trust my boss, or the company, or the system. That day marked the moment when I first thought, There has to be something better than this kind of trust.

The word "trust" is often used with words like "absolute," "assured," "unquestioning." Look at virtually any company in business today, and none of these words seem likely to be part of its corporate vocabulary.

Not too long ago, to distinguish itself from a longtime competitor, B. F. Goodrich advertised itself as the tire company without the blimp. More recently, the company began to differentiate itself in another way, running ads identifying itself as a company that no longer made tires.

Unable to compete profitably, B. F. Goodrich had sold its tire operations and now concentrated its efforts on businesses with greater potential for profit. Earnings per share doubled, Wall Street analysts commended the move, and the company's stock rose dramatically.

B. F. Goodrich obviously had made wise, profitable business decisions. After all, that's what corporations are supposed to do: compete effectively, improve profits, and increase shareholder value.

But B. F. Goodrich employees who had devoted fifteen or twenty years to making better tires may have viewed matters somewhat differently. Would they still have jobs? Would they have to look elsewhere? Would they need to learn new skills? Could the same thing happen again?

When the American Can Company determined that it had no future in cans, it left the business and changed its name to Primerica. When U.S. Steel considered the uncertain future of American steel making, it changed its name to USX Corp. Logo designers and corporate-identity consultants probably welcomed both decisions, but workers and managers at can factories and steel plants across the country were undoubtedly less enthusiastic.

Several years ago, Drake Beam Morin (DBM) was retained to help shut down an antiquated printing plant. I was at the facility on the day it closed for good, and I remember walking through the building soon after the last shift had departed. I wandered around, looking at presses and machinery that seemed old-fashioned and outdated even to my layman's eye.

But I noticed something else, too: a variety of chewing-gum and baling-wire improvements that employees had apparently dreamed up on their own to improve operations, or perhaps just to keep the plant running. I thought, If management had recognized the effort that had gone into these Rube Goldberg inventions, and had supported that effort with real resources, I wonder if this plant would have closed down today?

But even if the investment had been made, the lives of many employees would undoubtedly still have changed. Buy a new printing press, and half as many workers turn out twice as much printing. What happens to the idled employees?

When DBM assisted a large packaged-goods manufacturer in handling a major staff reduction, I talked with one of the line managers who would be responsible for terminating a number of employees. I knew that the manager had been on the receiving end of a similar program several years previously.

"You've been there," I said. "How will it feel to be on the other side of the process?"

"Well, I've given that a lot of thought," she said. "I'll never forget the shock and sadness and sense of betrayal we felt at my old company when the announcement came down that our division was going to close.

"But there's a difference. There, management waited and waited and did nothing, until there was only one choice: shut the whole thing down. Here they're trying to keep things going.

"Several of my people are going to take early retirement. Some of them are happy, and some aren't so sure. Some of my people are simply going to lose their jobs. I'm sorry about that, but not nearly as sorry as I was when I saw a whole company go down."

From the employee's point of view, the message seems to be "There's bad news and worse news." The bad news is that if the company does retrench, some people lose their jobs. The worse news is that if management does nothing and goes down, everyone loses a job.

What alternatives do companies have? In the 1950s and 1960s, American industry appeared to control its destiny. Growth was relatively steady, and jobs were relatively secure. There were layoffs, certainly, but they seemed manageable and temporary. If you worked on the assembly line in a General Motors factory and management discovered that it had built more Chevrolets than it could sell, you got laid off. But demand would eventually pick up again, and you'd be called back to work. You might spend your lunch break complaining about the company, but for the most part you could trust it.

By the late seventies, the rules had changed for good, and not everyone realized it. I remember sitting with a group of Ohio steelworkers who had recently been terminated. "What jobs are you looking into?" I asked one of the men.

"I want to go back to work at the mill," he said.

"But the mill's closed."

"It's been closed before."

The company had made it very clear that, this time, the mill had closed for good. Yet as I went around the room and talked to the men, I realized that most of them were going to wait it out in the hope that the plant would be reopened. It always had in the past, and they still trusted that, somehow, it would again in the future. I wonder how long it took them to abandon that trust.

Not long after that, I was in Detroit talking to a group of middle managers for one of the Big Three auto manufacturers. They had just learned about imminent layoffs within their own ranks, and they were shocked. Sure, layoffs were a traditional part of the auto business, but they were traditional to the factory floor. It just didn't happen to white-collar employees. Now that it did, was there anything left to trust?

[7]

It's been a tough couple of decades for the trust business. People may never have trusted individual politicians, but most did trust their government. That became more difficult following Watergate, Abscam, and Irangate. But if we couldn't trust our government, we had religion to rely on. The Bakkers and Jimmy Swaggert didn't make that any easier for some people. Well, if religion was no longer sacred, at least money was: we could still trust our representatives on Wall Street, with their rules and regulations and fiduciary responsibilities, to look after our dollars as if they were their own. And then some of our financial representatives decided that their needs really ought to come before ours. Well, at the very least, we could still trust the family. If we could find one that was still whole.

For many people, the one part of life left to rely on was the job. Here, at least, was something you could understand and perhaps even control. After all, through our jobs we know when to get up in the morning, what to wear, how to act, how to spend eight hours of the day, and, for many people, even who to look to for friendship. That could be reassuring, particularly when your broker was being indicted.

Once you figured out how your organization worked, you could get pretty good at understanding how and where you stood within it, what you could expect from it, and what the ground rules were.

There was a problem with this logic. As it turned out, we had even less control over our companies than we had had over those other unruly institutions. If we elected politicians, we could also vote them out of office (or watch as prosecutors took more direct action). If our congregation decided that the pastor wasn't up to snuff, we could find another. If a marriage didn't work out, we still might end up with half the assets. But most of us have never been in a position to impeach or divorce our companies. They don't work for us. We work for them.

They—in the form of top management—work for shareholders or boards of directors. And however much they honestly want employees to enjoy their jobs and feel a part of the family, they have other priorities.

Shareholders are a priority. The name of today's game is to create and improve shareholder value. That means, in essence, get the price of the company's stock to reflect the full value of the company's assets. It does not allow for hidebound thoughts like "Well, I know tires aren't that profitable for us anymore, but, for God's sake, we're a *tire* company!" Even if the whole company must be restructured, or the very nature of the business redefined, top management at one company after another is focused on this goal of improving shareholder value.

Part of the effort is undoubtedly prompted by a desire to be lean, mean, and productive, a welcome change in American business from only a few years ago. But there's another motivator, too: fear.

If current management can't do the job, a corporate raider or the merger-and-acquisition department of an investment bank is only too happy to help. One of the first things either force typically does to help is to install a new management team. Since top managers are no different from anyone else in at least one respect—they don't like getting fired either—they begin to think about "golden parachutes" and "poison pills," and to talk about "Pac-Man" defenses and "white knights."

Or they may engineer a leveraged buyout, putting up a relatively small amount of cash and taking on a relatively huge amount of debt, to buy the company back from the shareholders. The company's assets become the vehicle for paying off the debt. Some assets may be sold; all are likely to be examined to see how to make them cost the new owners less while producing more.

There can be an additional motivator behind the decision to pursue a leveraged buyout: greed. Tucked away in the huge debt may be millions, or tens of millions, or even hundreds of millions of dollars in bonuses and stock options that the management group awards itself for having the courage to make such a bold move. Most of these millions exist on paper at the start, however, and evaporate if the new company isn't successful. One more reason—a very personal reason—to cut, slash, and trim wherever possible.

2
CRADLE
TO GRAVE

Given the very real pressures that business and management face today, how can anyone feel secure in a job? No one is immune. When DBM is called on to help a company implement a downsizing, for instance, there normally comes a time when the client executives assigned to help manage the project begin to realize that some of them will very likely be included in the staff reduction.

The people at the top of the heap aren't immune. I remember talking to the chairman of one large company whose corporation had been targeted for a hostile takeover. Determined to fight the raid, he went looking for a white knight and found a company that seemed to offer a more compatible fit. The CEO persuaded that company's management to enter the bidding. It did, took control of the company, and, in one of its first moves, fired the CEO. He was shocked.

I wasn't that surprised: the handwriting on the wall had seemed perfectly legible. Perhaps the man had been simply unwilling to read it, a reaction that may be the vocational equivalent of whistling in the dark: if you don't hear the bogeyman, he won't get you. With our jobs, that becomes the unrealistic belief that, although it's happening everywhere, *it just won't happen here.*

If you ask someone, "Do you believe that 'cradle-to-grave' employment exists in the U.S. today?" you get a funny look.

"Certainly not!" you're told. "That went out in the fifties, or certainly in the sixties."

But when people are pushed out of that cradle before

reaching the grave, the reaction is likely to be different: "How could this happen to me?"

More important questions deserve answers. Where did we get the idea that we could trust the company to take care of us? How did the image of the company as the nurturing, all-providing parent become established in America? How, in the face of overwhelming evidence to the contrary, has it persisted?

Perhaps the cradle-to-grave philosophy was an over-reaction to the very real problems and dangers associated with employment in the nineteenth and early twentieth centuries. The horrors of child labor and dangerous work-place conditions, tragedies like the Triangle factory fire, the battles and victories of labor unions, all these finally pushed government and business to consider the impact of the work environment on the worker.

Management began to realize that a better environment for the worker could result in a better product and greater productivity. If better lighting conditions meant that people wouldn't mangle their hands in the machinery, it also meant they could do more work. If giving people a regular day off, or even a full weekend, meant that they would be less likely to fall asleep on the job, well, that might help the product, too. As the man on the shop floor moved toward a forty-hour week and a paid vacation, the clerks and bookkeepers in the office demanded similar benefits.

It wasn't too great a step from better lighting to medical and life insurance. These benefits could be justified because they relieved employee concerns about their families and futures, and thus permitted the individual to perform at an even higher level of commitment and productivity. But at some point the employer crossed a line that clearly defined the employer-employee relationship, and an element of paternalism began to intrude.

At most American corporations today, a huge variety of benefits come attached to a management position. Your family's medical, and perhaps dental, expenses will be covered to one degree or another. Profit sharing and a pension plan will figure into your retirement plans. You may be given retirement counseling to help you plan for that future. You could drive a company car. You might drive it to a company country club. (Or you may be given a company membership to another club.) You'll have a company life insurance policy. If you have to move to a new location, your company may provide relocation assistance, or help with a new mortgage. If your spouse needs to find a new job in the new location, the company may help with employment counseling.

Since both you and your spouse are likely to be employed today, your company may provide child care for your young children. Or grants, scholarships, or tuition assistance for college-bound offspring. Your tuition may be paid if you continue your own education. If you give money to a charity, your company may match your gift.

You may play on a company-sponsored softball team. Or seek assistance from company-sponsored counseling programs if you or your family encounter trouble with substance abuse, have trouble in your marriage, or need help with your finances. You may spend your lunch hour in a subsidized cafeteria or restaurant, and you may work off the meal in the company health club.

If you work for an old-fashioned company, you might still attend a company picnic. Or receive a turkey at Christmas.

Even if the worst does happen and you get fired, the benefits don't end. Your company pays you severance and hires companies like mine to offer career-continuation counseling to get you back to work in a new position.

All these benefits are enlightened and well-intentioned.

After all, who can quarrel with things like good health or education? But in sum, they encourage the employee to look at the employer as the great provider. And it isn't too great a step from being the great provider of benefits to being viewed as the eternal provider of employment—the continual paycheck, from cradle to grave.

As companies continually expanded their rosters of benefits, what did they expect in return? After all, people can only work so many hours each day. Once the limit is reached, what else can the employee give to the company? Trust. The commitment to stick things out in good times and bad, to give one's all, to be totally devoted to the company. In the psychological exchange of loyalty for benefits, the cradle-to-grave concept was born.

As this exchange was becoming grounded in the corporate culture, another shift was taking place as well, as America moved from a small-shop, agrarian economy to an industrial society. An entirely new culture was created.

In an agrarian society, you helped your neighbors and they helped you. They helped build your barn, and you helped harvest their crops. But ultimately you were responsible for yourself. You raised your own food and worked toward self-sufficiency. If you failed, you lost the farm, a fate that has never been foreign to the rural population.

It's different in a factory or an office tower. You're part of the equipment. You're not self-sufficient. You depend on what comes along the assembly line or down the organizational pyramid. If you install carburetors, your work is only as good as that of all the other parts installers. If you create marketing plans, you're probably pretty far removed from the real market. It becomes difficult to see yourself as separate from the company, to see yourself as an individual.

In an agrarian society, every planting season brings a

new beginning. You literally start from scratch. Bad years may follow good ones, and your hope is that everything will even out in the end. But in industry, the more time you put into "the company," the more benefits you accrue: more seniority, higher pay, longer vacations, a bigger pension, a larger office. The underlying message is "Keep feeding us, and we'll keep feeding you." It's easy to see how this system nourishes loyalty to a particular company, the idea that, if you stay with the company, the company will stay with you.

And throughout the fifties and sixties, the promise was likely to be kept. What, after all, was so wrong with the notion that "What's good for General Motors is good for America"?

As companies were refining the cradle-to-grave philosophy, they were also promoting other corporate ideals. One was the idea that the corporation is larger than life, that it takes on a life of its own, that, regardless of competition or product quality, it's just too big to stop. That could be reassuring to workers. If nothing could stop the company, what could threaten their jobs?

By the seventies, the plot had begun to unravel, beginning with substantial plant layoffs. Reacting to this trend, unions negotiated job security clauses into their contracts. Workers and management were on a collision course.

At first the situation seemed manageable, as only the most recently hired individuals were terminated, while seniority protected long-term employees. This kept the noise level down. In addition, many companies protected redundant executives with a process called "shelving." Ranks of senior executives with virtually no responsibilities continued to collect large salaries, receive extensive benefits, and create tremendous top-heaviness in corporate America.

By the late 1970s, the combination of tight money, high

interest rates, and stiff foreign competition forced industry's hand. We've all witnessed the results as one industry after another paid the piper.

For many people, this radical process restructuring led to a complete disaffection with American industry. Study after study indicates that as few as 20 percent of American workers are willing to call themselves loyal employees anymore.

But if people are no longer loyal, why do they continue to be surprised when a company cuts them loose? The answer, I think, may lie in the findings of an internal survey conducted by a leading American corporation. In this survey, researchers learned that, while the company's employees overwhelmingly trusted the company, they overwhelmingly distrusted its management.

That may be the key. We still need to trust something, so we call it the company. Perhaps that's our vision of business as we think it was twenty years ago, or industry as we've been told it's supposed to be: fair play, honest competition, Jack Armstrong. None of it may actually have ever been true, but we need to believe it to get on with our lives and our careers.

At the same time, we're not fools. If it's not the company that's at fault, it must be those guys running it. Think for a moment. Do you trust your management?

3

NEW RULES AND OLD LOYALTY

PICTURE THIS. A manager interviews for a new job. He thinks the interviewer is friendly and considerate—which she is: professionally considerate and friendly. She's skilled at putting people at ease to get them to reveal facts they might otherwise guard. She's doing her job and doing it well, but should our job-seeker trust her?

Picture this. He gets the job and starts work. He's met everyone in the department during the interview process and thinks they're terrific. They want him here; they've told him so. The sky's the limit regarding opportunities for advancement; they've told him that, as well. This is a team effort, an aggressive team effort; he's heard that, too. He'll be an important part of that team.

His new boss is genuinely interested in what the man thinks and feels. This is a place where he can grow and prosper. He's found himself a home.

A month later, he's not so sure. His colleagues treat him warily. They seem more interested in their own turf than in destroying the competitors. Does he trust these people?

His boss hasn't turned out to be quite the friend he'd imagined. The new man isn't his first loyalty: the boss is concerned with business.

Six months later, the man is worried. The competition has refused to roll over. Instead, they've beaten his team to market with a new product. There are rumors about changes in the department and a restructuring throughout the division. The boss calls him into his office.

"I don't know how to tell you this," he tells the man, "and I want you to know this certainly wasn't my idea..."

Why did he ever trust this man?

He trusted him because he played by the old rules: do your job, keep your head down, get along, and trust that you'll be taken care of. Today there's a different set of rules.

Rule 1:
There is no such thing as job security.

Today, reputable companies don't guarantee continued employment to new—or old—employees. The current trend is this: You're hired to do a specific job at a specific salary, with certain benefits. If you do the job well—and if your colleagues and superiors do their jobs well—you may be employed for a long time. Do the job poorly—or choose a company where others do their jobs poorly, or where business suddenly turns down—and the company won't hesitate to fire you.

This corporate mind-set has given rise to a new employment concept that is the antithesis of job longevity and career security: employee "leasing." There are companies today, Drake Beam Morin included, that offer other companies "management à la carte" by supplying them with experienced executives on a project basis.

A company needs help with its marketing strategy for a new product. Rather than hire someone (and incur the expense of search costs and employee benefits—or have to contend with an implicit promise of permanent employment), the company hires a high-level "temp" for the duration of the assignment.

We've discovered that many of our clients appreciate such opportunities. Some have reached the decision to return to the marketplace as consultants. They want to work for themselves, guide their own destinies, and not put themselves at the mercy of management again. Other clients do intend to return to permanent jobs, and find

that a temporary assignment can give them a foot in the
door. By demonstrating their abilities on the assignment
they've been retained to complete, they improve their
chances of being offered permanent employment.

Rule 2:
**You are responsible for your career—its planning,
direction, and progress.**

Companies have little time or inclination to provide
employees with career counseling today, or even to ex-
pose them to a variety of career choices. They look for
people who, beginning with their first day on the job, will
contribute to the bottom line.

Today's successful employee combines excellent work
skills with the desire and ability to contribute at a high
level of efficiency. Such employees are constantly learning new skills and acquiring knowledge in their fields.
Even if such training or education isn't provided by the
company, these individuals are willing to make the investment on their own.

Successful employees examine their own performance
continually. What's the purpose of what I'm doing? they
may ask. Am I making a real contribution? What am I
learning that I can use in the future? Am I doing this for
my boss, or for the business? (The two are often not the
same.)

This self-examination provides the successful employee
with a valuable knowledge of his or her accomplishments.

When people enter DBM career-continuation programs, one of the first tasks we ask them to do is to list
their career accomplishments. Our consultants have
learned to expect a common reaction to the assignment:
"I don't really have any . . . I just haven't done much with
my life."

There's something about the corporate identity that

masks individual accomplishments. People say, "Well, it was really the boss's idea," or "The whole team was involved; my role was pretty minor," or "I just did what they told me." When we probe these individuals, however, they find themselves able to create long lists of solid accomplishments.

Rule 3:
Knowing what the company expects of you is *your* responsibility.

When you're hired today, or change assignments within your company, or get a new boss, or encounter any situation that makes you suspect that the ground rules have changed, it's up to you to determine what's expected of you. It seems obvious that your manager should share such information with you as clearly as possible, but very often managers do a less-than-perfect job of communicating.

When DBM career-continuation clients are offered new jobs, our consultants insist that, to discover whether it's the *right* job, they determine exactly what their responsibilities will be. This seems only natural. But even then, when a client accepts a new position, the details of which he or she has investigated carefully already, the DBM consultant makes a suggestion.

"Your first day on the job, sit down with your boss and go over your responsibilities one more time."

"But why?" the client asks. "I've gone through that already."

"Do me a favor," the consultant says. "Sit down with your boss and two pieces of paper. Ask your boss to list the five things you ought to do first. Write down your own list of five priorities."

The odds are that no more than two items will appear on both lists.

Under the old psychological contract, where you were led to believe that it was the company's job to look after you, it was reasonable to expect that, if management wanted you to know something, you'd hear about it. But today the company expects you to understand your duties and what's expected of you. Period. The burden's on you.

Loyalty just isn't what it used to be. But what is?

There was a time when management expected unquestioning loyalty from employees.

"We're reassigning you to the North Dakota office," you were told.

"Fine, I'll have my wife get the cold-weather clothes out of storage," you responded.

Companies acted this way because it seemed that they gave their employees a pretty good deal built around job security. But, as with employees, today the rules have changed for management, too.

"We have a great new job for you in Florida," you're told.

"It's too hot down there," you answer. "Besides, my wife and kids would never leave North Dakota."

Lacking the ability to dangle the carrot of real job security, management has found it's gotten harder to wave a stick for undying employee loyalty.

Expectation management, or value management, are new buzzwords in corporate circles. Employees should know what's expected of them. Management should know what value it needs to get from employees. There has to be clear, two-way communication. The days of blind loyalty are gone.

But again and again, the word "loyalty" emerges in conversations about work.

"People just aren't loyal anymore."

"Fifteen years with the company, and she jumps ship to

start her own business! I thought she was loyal."

"He worked for me for six years, and we were very close. All of a sudden, he's leaving to take another job. He never told me a thing. There's no loyalty anymore."

Clearly, the old loyalty just doesn't fit today's work environment. What we need is a new corporate loyalty.

4

THE NEW
CORPORATE
LOYALTY

A CONTRACT OR AGREEMENT, written or assumed, takes effect when a company hires you. You agree to work for the company, and in return the company agrees to pay you for as long as it uses your services.

A contract isn't a personal relationship, although we often confuse the two. Phrases that have one meaning in a personal relationship—"You have my word" or "Let's shake on it"—may have entirely different implications in a profit-motivated business setting.

But all relationships have at least one thing in common, whether they involve friends or relatives, employers, bosses, or subordinates. To be successful, they depend on communication and negotiation. What varies is the extent to which we put our own needs first.

In personal relationships, we may give of ourselves to prompt a similar response. That response becomes our "payment," and in good relationships we expect to receive about the same emotional payment as we invest over time. Ideally, the more we share, care, and love, the more we're shared with, cared for, and loved.

It's understandable to try to bring this same dynamic into the workplace, but experience suggests that things don't work the same way on the job. In the workplace, our first loyalty has to be to our own needs. I come first. You come first to yourself. We all come first for ourselves. It sounds selfish, but it's really an expression of selfness, the cornerstone of what I call non-dependent trust. Non-dependent trust takes our natural desire to trust others and fits that inclination to the business environment.

The key difference between the two settings, personal

and professional, is that in corporate America a person doesn't employ you, a company does. Your company isn't a living person but an economic and legal entity with priorities that, at times, are almost certain to be at odds with your needs.

A company has two goals—to be profitable and to grow—and one underlying constraint—to achieve these objectives within the law. Anything else, from supporting the local symphony to looking out for employees' future, is ultimately superfluous in corporate terms and may be sacrificed to those central goals. A company doesn't have feelings or emotions or, if we're honest about it, an intrinsic responsibility to society. Its ultimate responsibility is to its owners or stockholders.

Company managers or board members do have feelings, of course, and these feelings often find their way into corporate culture. Some business leaders, worried about the consequences of making shareholder value the only determinant of corporate strategy, have proposed that the interests of "stakeholders," the people who work for the company, or who live in the towns and cities where it operates, should also be weighed when company decisions are made.

But—today at any rate—you probably still work for a legal entity, not a caring individual. You certainly hope your managers and superiors care about you, but you also need to recognize the implications of the contract—formal or implicit—that exists between you and your company, and that is implemented by you and your immediate superior, your boss or manager.

Your boss should guide you in your duties, which you must perform adequately or better. The relationship can be one-sided: even if your boss isn't a great guide, you're still expected to perform. And there isn't a lot of room for negotiation. If you can't perform your duties, your boss may choose to train you or dismiss you. For the company to pursue its objectives, your boss should make such decisions with the company's best interests in mind. So at some point the overriding, impersonal needs of the company take over.

And at some point closer to home, your manager's personal needs are likely to take precedence over your own needs. If your boss is to adopt the notion of non-dependent trust, after all, his or her needs will have to take precedence over yours.

What can happen? Your manager promises you a raise, but a corporate wage freeze is announced, and now she can't deliver. You expect and deserve a promotion, but your manager tells you that, because of an employee downsizing, you might be lucky to have *any* job next month. Your manager hears about upcoming cutbacks, doesn't inform you because of a management directive demanding secrecy, and leaves the company for another job. None of these actions is the work of an unethical, unworthy person. Yet they reinforce the value, or perhaps the necessity, of putting your own interests first.

So your first loyalty is to yourself. But this doesn't mean that you have no responsibilities to the company or to your colleagues. In fact, focusing on the difference between loyalty and responsibility can help you become an outstanding employee.

Loyalty is unquestioning. Responsibility demands that you analyze the situation and make decisions based on your analysis. When you carry out your boss's directions without question, you're being loyal. You may also be acting totally irresponsibly.

Responsible employees think about the tasks they are asked to perform by asking themselves some questions:

- Does this instruction make sense to me?

- Is this instruction compatible with similar tasks I've done in the past?

- Do I understand my instructions well enough to complete the task?

- Do I know how my performance will be measured?

- Do I understand how my performance will be rewarded?

Answer No to any of these questions, and it's your responsibility to discuss the situation with your manager. This can obviously be a difficult task, since most people don't particularly like to have their ideas challenged or orders questioned. It's certainly not appropriate to always question everything, but I'm convinced that more trouble is caused by not asking such questions than by raising them.

In a recent survey conducted by Drake Beam Morin for a billion-dollar company, the majority of employees stated that they believed in the values of their corporation. But 70 percent of the respondents said they didn't trust management to run the business properly. A majority also felt very confused about what was expected of them. Such attitudes are on the increase in America today, more the rule than the exception. In this kind of environment, it becomes more and more important for someone to ask the right questions. Trust yourself to do so. It might be the only way to survive in the 1990s and beyond.

In an ideal world, of course, there would only be ideal managers, who, thinking constantly about issues like the ones raised above, would see to it that your questions were answered, and that you were optimally equipped and prepared to perform your job. In the real world, life is somewhat different, but the goal should be the same. If we are to approach that goal via the non-dependent trust route, guess whose responsibility it is to see that the questions are asked, and answered, so that the job can be performed. Yours.

How can you frame such a dialogue? Perhaps the best way is to think in terms of expectation management. Your company and your manager have the right to expect certain things from you. You, in return, can expect certain things from them. In this real world of ours, a range of personal needs, special interests, differing communication styles, and hidden agendas make agreeing to these expectations anything but simple. But suppose we could strip away these competing forces for a moment. What would a set of "proper" expectations look like, for employees, managers, and the company? See the Expectation Checklist on page 34.

EXPECTATION CHECKLIST

Company Expectations of Employees	Manager Expectations of Employees	Employee Expectations of Company	Employee Expectations of Manager
Comes in on time.	Carries out tasks in efficient and attentive manner.	Provides safe, comfortable work environment.	Explains job tasks clearly.
Puts in a full workday in a productive manner.	Understands parameters of job and works within these guidelines.	Pursues business policies that lead to corporate growth and financial stability.	Is available to employee for questions and directions.
Maintains positive work attitude.	Keeps manager informed on business matters as necessary.	Pays employee on time, and at agreed amount.	Wants employee to succeed.
As much as possible, supports and believes in company's product and services.	Comes to manager with questions and concerns.	Pursues policies that foster health, e.g., providing vacation time.	Keeps employee informed about the state of the business.
Thinks about the business and is willing to make suggestions for improvement in a positive manner.	Gives manager feedback on improving products and service.	Provides opportunities for advancement and learning.	Evaluates performance on a fair and timely basis.
Is helpful to co-workers.	Keeps up to date with changes in the profession.	Keeps employee informed of the state of the business.	Sets reasonable goals and objectives and seeks consent of the employee.
Has limited amount of personal time and sick days.	Does not spread news to co-workers of conflicts with manager.	Does not defame the employee or act in an intimidating way.	Performs job coaching rather than simply evaluating the employee's performance.
Continues to develop career and job skills on his/her own.	Keeps manager informed on personal matters as they affect the business.	Informs employee on all matters that could affect the employee's career.	Respects the dignity of the employee.

No doubt about it, these expectation guidelines are optimistic and idealistic. They will not be rammed down anyone's throat, boss or subordinate. But they can serve as a valuable discussion guide for a conversation between you and your boss, or between you and your subordinate. If you, the subordinate, can meet these expectations, you're a responsible employee. If the company and/or your manager aren't keeping their part of the bargain, you need to look for ways to express your concerns in a positive fashion. If there is no way to do that, you may need to look elsewhere for employment.

Even if you and your company do meet these expectations, the job of being a responsible employee involves thinking about the future, both for the business and for yourself. Just as your company probably has a business plan that looks one, two, or five years into the future, so should you look ahead by making a personal business plan of your own. After all, *you* are a business that sells certain skills and services to your employer. If you don't plan ahead, you might go out of business.

An important aspect of this personal plan is to forecast the kinds of skills you'll need for the future, either for your present job or in the broader job market. If everyone in your business is switching to computer operations and you're still "illiterate" in the field, it's probably time to take a computer course at a local college. If technology threatens to make your job obsolete, it's time to investigate adapting your skills to another industry. Perhaps nothing appears to be changing in your business, but you haven't read a professional book in three years. That can be a danger signal. No job is forever, and you're the only person who can sharpen your own skills continually. No one else is going to assure your ability to compete in a constantly changing job market.

Here are ten survival questions to ask yourself:

1. Am I making a real contribution?

2. Do I understand what's expected of me on the job?

3. Are my expectations in sync with those of the company, my boss, and my peers?

4. Do I know what the end results of my efforts should be?

5. Do I have a clear understanding of how these results are perceived and appraised by my boss?

6. Have I recently added anything to my general knowledge of the business or to the skills I have to offer?

7. Am I reaching out for new professional skills? Am I growing?

8. Am I careful about limiting the amount of time I spend on personal business during office hours?

9. Do I have a personal business plan for my career?

10. Am I thinking about the business?

If you can answer Yes to these questions, you're a prime practitioner of the new corporate loyalty.

Finally, complete the Personal Business Plan chart that follows. It can help you focus on what you expect of your job and your future. In column 1 (My Needs Today), use a scale of 1 to 10 to weight each of the criteria according to how important each factor is in terms of your current career needs. Then, in column 2, weight each factor, again on a scale of 1 to 10, in terms of how well your current job satisfies your career needs. Compare to see where differences exist. Then, in columns 3, 4, and 5, project your expectations of future needs one, two, and four years into the future.

Few people ever plan their careers. You can and you should. Trust yourself!

PERSONAL BUSINESS PLAN

Criteria	My Needs Today	Current Job	My Needs in One Year	My Needs in Two Years	My Needs in Four Years
CAREER/PROFESSIONAL					
Accountability					
Adequacy of My Staff					
Title					
Promotion/Growth Potential					
Decision-Making Authority					
COMPANY					
Size of Company					
Company Characteristics					
Management Style					
PERSONAL					
Compensation Base					
Bonus/Profit Sharing, etc.					
Benefits					
Perks					
Geographic Location					
Travel Requirements					
Commuting Requirements					
Special Expenses					
TOTALS					

If your scores in column 2 fall between:

16–56   Your job satisfaction is dangerously low and you might want to consider new employment.

57–80   Your job satisfaction is a little below average and you may want to discuss with your immediate supervisor how some of your needs can be better met.

81–120   Your job satisfaction is quite high and you have obviously chosen the right job with a bright future.

121–160 Your job satisfaction is exemplary and you must be the envy of your colleagues.

5
NON-DEPENDENT
TRUST

THE KEY TO NON-DEPENDENT TRUST is that—as an individual and as a professional—you must care for yourself and assume responsibility for your future. No longer do you look to the company, or your boss, or your colleagues or friends for a ready-made sense of security. Instead, you realize that you're the only one who can create and maintain a personal scenario for happiness and success. This can involve planning your career, keeping abreast of developments in your field, staying alert to opportunities inside and outside your company, and managing your work-related responsibilities thoughtfully and to the best of your abilities. Not a new concept, but one few of us embrace.

Non-dependent trust does *not* involve thinking that no one matters but you. It doesn't mean walking away from your responsibilities with a "What-the-hell!" attitude. It's not playing your cards close to your vest. It's not blaming the company for your own failures, and it certainly doesn't involve ignoring your responsibility to continually perform as effectively as you can. (When you're at work, do you concentrate 100 percent of your energy on the job? Some observers indicate that managers and employees spend as much as 30 percent of the workday on things other than business.)

Non-dependent trust thrives on honesty. Wherever possible, you must level with your manager and your company: state your needs, ask questions about your future, find out what's expected of you, press for frequent evaluations of your performance, air your grievances, and, most of all, recognize that you are the one who is most responsible for your own well-being.

This focus on honesty should permeate every aspect of your relationship with your company. But not all companies, and not all bosses, appreciate such candor. Consider the complications that non-dependent trust might create for just one hallowed business institution, the expense account. Like parents confronted with the opportunity to discuss sex with their adolescent children, many managers avoid discussing the topic with their subordinates entirely, reasoning, "This person is an adult. He can figure it out." That isn't always the case.

In 1963, soon after I graduated from college, as I was about to depart on the first business trip of my career, I had no idea how to handle my expenses. I asked my boss for guidance.

"Bill," he told me, "the whole idea is to live on the road as you would at home." And then he changed the subject.

It made no sense to me then, and it makes no sense now. But I know that the same "advice" continues to be offered today. Less than a year ago, an executive at a major corporation told me that his company embraced the same philosophy.

My company didn't know whether I breakfasted on cold toast or poached pheasant eggs at home. How was I supposed to act on the road? What if I went on a trip with a fellow employee who spent thirty dollars for his dinner, while I only spent twenty dollars for mine? What if our manager routinely approved both expense reports? Should I have thought I was losing out on a ten-dollar company benefit? The next time out, might I be tempted to spend twenty, write down thirty, and pocket the difference?

It happens all the time, of course. Rather than give me the receipts printed by their meters, taxi drivers rummage through their cabs to find blank receipts, which they hand me with a wink. After I pay for a meal, tip the waiter or waitress, and ask for a receipt, I'm asked, "How much should I make out your receipt for?"

When you go out with your boss for a meal or a drink, who pays? Frequently it's the subordinate. If the boss pays and submits an expense claim, the next higher boss just might ask, "Was this really a legitimate business expense?" To avoid such an uncomfortable situation, the subordinate pays and then includes the item on an expense report that goes, conveniently enough, to his or her guest/boss. The boss approves the expense, and everyone's happy.

Companies may turn a blind eye to such practices. One senior manager even told me, "Oh, we know he's been playing with his expenses all along. We once reimbursed him for dinner at two different restaurants on the same night. That's OK. He has an employment contract, and if we ever want to break it, we'll show him his expense reports and suggest that it might be best for all parties if he simply resigned."

The waiters and taxi drivers are trying to do me a favor, my boss and I may get a free drink, and companies may have their own agendas, but what does it all say about the trust relationship between ourselves and our companies?

What's the alternative? Should you go to your boss and say, "Look, we need a realistic policy on expenses around here. People aren't sure what to do, the company is losing dollars, and we could all focus on our real jobs—and not worry about how much to put in for—if we had a consistent set of rules"? Will the world, or your company, love a straight arrow or a whistle-blower? The office is a jungle, after all. Isn't this just a bit idealistic?

Yes, it is idealistic, and the world is not as neat and orderly as we might like. But to understand non-dependent trust, and to make it work for us by making it an operative principle of our work lives, we need to develop workplace values and visualize where we'd like to go with our careers. Then we can apply some of these concepts to the "jungle" reality of the modern American workplace.

We need to be realistic, of course. If industry publications and the business section of your local newspaper indicate that your industry is going through a slump or that your company is a prime prospect on some raider's list of potential takeovers, it's probably not a good time to confront your boss with questions about future career opportunities. If your department is struggling to finish off a crash project, it's obviously not the time to raise expense policies as the crucial issue of the hour.

We all need to be sensitive to our work environment. In the jungle, you don't attack a lion with a toy gun. This not only helps us avoid making serious judgment errors, but it also helps maintain a realistic view of our situation, one of the key requirements of non-dependent trust. Perhaps the simplest way to develop this awareness is to keep eyes and ears open, nurture channels of communication in all directions, and think before speaking or acting. It sounds simple, but few people apply such principles successfully in the work environment.

Companies can—and should—help. Non-dependent trust from a corporate management point of view means giving employees enough information to operate effectively in the workplace and take charge of their own careers. This includes creating an environment in which workers can easily learn about career opportunities, about the fiscal health of the company, and about the organization's long-range plans, so that they can be responsible, aware employees.

Non-dependent trust also requires that employees have a safe opportunity to tell management what the company needs to hear—not what it wants to hear. This means creating open lines of communication at all levels of the organization and seeing to it that the information that flows along these lines is taken seriously. It means assuring employees that they have a stake in the operation of the company and a responsibility to view that interest thoughtfully. Non-dependent trust means delegating authority by letting people make meaningful decisions. Methods for accomplishing these ends can range from archaic suggestion boxes to the latest trend in quality circles. The company's *commitment* to open communication is perhaps more important than its methods.

Companies that have a non-dependent trust relationship with their employees pay for performance, not for looking good. If the company is to perform its role—creating growth and profits—it has to demand performance. Think about your company. Does its incentive plan really pay for performance? Are merit raises really based on merit?

Perhaps the most important aspect of non-dependent trust from the corporation's point of view is the understanding that companies are in a partnership with employees. To be successful, this partnership requires the goodwill of the participants, the acknowledgment of mutual goals and responsibilities, and the willingness to communicate openly. In a tough business climate, it may well be the existence of such a partnership, rather than a particular product or marketing plan, that determines a company's ultimate success or failure.

6

A MANAGER'S GUIDE TO NON-DEPENDENT TRUST

CORPORATE SHEEP! I've got a company full of corporate sheep!" the CEO complained. "They follow instructions—any instructions! But there's no initiative, no creativity. They don't ask questions. They don't make suggestions. They just mill around and graze for paychecks.

"But, you know, it's funny," he continued. "Even though they follow orders, I don't think they really trust management to do the right thing. And I certainly wouldn't trust any of them to implement anything critical. How can I get this company back on track?"

This CEO's dilemma was fueled by a common management failure: forgetting that a company's lifeblood rests with individual employees and their ability to analyze, criticize, and be creative. At his company, management had decided it was high time to revive corporate "loyalty," a value that—as at many other American companies in the early eighties—had suffered mightily when business downturns necessitated staff cutbacks and tough union negotiations.

The company stressed the idea that employees should "pull together, speak the same language, become one unit." What management apparently forgot was that, by demanding that everyone toe the company line, it became nearly impossible for employees to think and operate independently.

Over time, employees with independent points of view, those who were willing to question and challenge management, were weeded out of the organization. Or they removed themselves voluntarily. The sheep remained.

The greatest waste in American business today involves people and their ideas: ideas that are lost, opportunities missed, improvements that could have been made if management had listened to its employees.

By contrast, when a company creates an environment in which people feel free to make suggestions, and where they know that their contributions will be listened to with respect, employees tend to be loyal, creative, and supportive. Even when their ideas are impractical, simply having the contribution acknowledged lets employees know that they are contributing to the company. They gain a sense of ownership and feel free to offer additional suggestions in the future.

An unrelenting stream of lip service has been paid to this idea, but model situations are scarce. Companies institute special employee participation or recognition programs when it's already too late to take advantage of any ideas that might come out of them. As the programs fail, and as employees leave the company—often to work for competitors—management asks, "Whatever happened to company loyalty?"

What happened usually occurred over a period of years, as management broke its trust contract by refusing to solicit and listen to employee ideas. No longer able to promise cradle-to-grave employment, and never having built a feeling among employees that they had a real stake in the business of running the company, the company had a weak foundation on which to build trust or ask for loyalty.

It doesn't have to be that way. Companies can create and nurture non-dependent trust in the workplace. Probably the most crucial individual in making non-dependent trust work is the front-line manager, the person with the greatest opportunity to establish and maintain a trust environment on a day-to-day basis.

Managers who wish to create such an environment need to concentrate on their relationships with employees who report directly to them. A simple four-point action plan for building solid relationships with employees can benefit both the company *and* the individual employee, and can set a model for other managers to emulate.

A key premise behind this plan is that lapses in the trust relationship most often occur because management and employees, knowingly or otherwise, work from different "rule books." Neither really knows what the other expects.

Management can improve the situation by attending to four basic priorities:

1. Determine and clearly communicate to employees the company's management policies and philosophies.

2. Explain how the employee is expected to operate within the company's culture.

3. State the employee's job responsibilities clearly, and discuss the criteria for performance evaluation that these responsibilities dictate.

4. Make no promises that give employees a false sense of well-being.

Let's look at these four priorities in detail.

(1) Communicate Company Policy

At a recent conference, I asked top executives from sixty major international corporations to write down their companies' policies or management philosophies regarding employees. They couldn't do it.

Most sat and stared out the window or at each other. Later, in small-group discussions, nearly all of the executives referred back to this exercise. None was able to say just what his or her company believed in, what the corporation thought about trust and loyalty. Did management trust its employees? Was loyalty important to the company? They didn't seem to know, but they did feel that they ought to.

While this lack of well-defined, clearly communicated management philosophy is anything but rare, it need not be. Consider Johnson & Johnson's well-known example of a well-articulated corporate policy:

JOHNSON & JOHNSON CREDO

- We are responsible to our employees, the men and women who work with us throughout the world.

- Everyone must be considered an individual.

- We must recognize their dignity and recognize their merit. They must have a sense of security in their jobs.

- Compensation must be fair and adequate, and working conditions clean, orderly, and safe.

- Employees must feel free to make suggestions and complaints.

- There must be equal opportunity for employment, development, and advancement for those qualified.

- We must provide competent management, and their actions must be just and ethical.

This credo clearly outlines the company's responsibilities to the worker, and the worker's obligations to the company. It emphasizes management's concern for a workplace in which ethical behavior is valued. Without mentioning the words trust or loyalty, it describes a situation in which both can flourish. Employees have clear guidelines for measuring their own behavior, that of their colleagues, and of the company as a whole. The Johnson & Johnson credo is an excellent model for both corporate and employee behavior.

The Drake Beam Morin Code is our organization's attempt to define the things we think are important to our clients, ourselves, and our business. The ideas expressed in the code are fundamental, even obvious. But substantial thought and effort went into its creation. Realizing that we were committing ourselves to these values, we considered each one carefully before etching it in stone.

DRAKE BEAM MORIN CODE

Clients will receive:

- Complete respect.

- Assistance and guidance only after we hear and understand their questions.

- What was agreed to and more, but never less than was agreed—or their fees will be refunded.

- The highest quality services available as compared to industry standards.

- The best services at the most competitive prices available.

- The truth, to the best of DBM's ability.

- Understanding, support, and a genuine effort to establish friendship.

Employees will be:

- Required to perform to the best of their ability.

- Expected to treat the company as they want to be treated.

- Given authority over—and held accountable for—practice development, practice furtherance, and client satisfaction.

- Recognized for who they are and appreciated for the contribution they make.

- Trusted to do what is best for themselves and for the company.

- Treated fairly by management.

- Encouraged to take risks and allowed to make mistakes.

- Coached rather than criticized.

- Motivated by opportunity and by example rather than fear.

- Rewarded for professional excellence in accordance with DBM compensation and incentive plans.

(2) Transmit the Corporate Culture

Creating a code like ours represents a conscious attempt to institutionalize the more formal pieces of our company culture, the practices, customs, and beliefs that characterize the way we approach our business.

Whether it promotes the idea or not, every company has a corporate culture. And, since this culture distinguishes between acceptable behavior and inappropriate activity, and potential success from failure, employees who are going to prosper—or even survive—in the company need to be attuned to these values.

Written codes, and credos framed on office walls, can help the situation, but the details of a corporate culture, which might never be articulated or publicized, can be just as important. That's where experienced managers can support their employees, guiding them through the reefs and shoals of unwritten company expectations.

Consider something as basic and obvious as business dress. Take ten employees from a West Coast computer software firm and put them in a room with ten representatives of an East Coast investment bank. You'll have no trouble telling the two groups apart. Each group will look precisely the way software people or investment bankers are supposed to look.

But what happens if one of the investment bankers starts coming to work dressed like a software designer—in an open-collared, short-sleeved shirt with a plastic pencil case in the breast pocket, perhaps? What shape will his career path take?

Or what if the software company decides that its employees should start dressing like investment bankers? Where are its employees likely to head?

One well-known company nearly put itself out of business by mandating that all male employees wear knee-length socks to work. The employees decided that the company didn't trust them to manage their own wardrobes. In response, they didn't trust that the company was honestly concerned about their needs, or even about the company's own best interests. How could they be, if they were so concerned about such corporate minutiae? Shouldn't top management be interested in knocking the socks off the competition rather than checking the socks of its employees?

Such issues seem petty, but they can be important. If you are a very aggressive individual, for example, but your company's style is restrained and non-confrontational, your nature may make you a top producer or contributor, but your style might block you at every turn.

"He's not a member of the team," your associates could say, or "He's just not our type."

Not only are you blocked as a result, but the company is as well. It doesn't fully benefit from your contributions.

In a situation like this, a sensitive manager might coach you to help you adapt your behavior to company norms. You might decide that you don't want to change your style, a decision that could lead you to another, more compatible company. Indeed, that definitive course of action might be more productive for both you and your current employer.

(3) Explain Responsibilities and Performance Criteria

If your manager helps you understand your company's culture, you gain a good idea of how to approach your work. To perform successfully, however—both for yourself and for the company—you obviously also need to know *what* you should be doing and how you'll be evaluated for your performance. So a critical aspect of developing non-dependent trust relationships with subordinates involves the manager's ability to explain job responsibilities and evaluation criteria. Many managers fail miserably at this task.

Consider this common refrain: "When I was hired, my manager told me, 'Just jump in. The job is yours to create.' I was never given any real guidelines, and I was eventually fired for not 'doing my job.' But, even on the day I got fired, no one could tell me exactly what it was that they'd wanted me to do, or exactly where it was that I went wrong."

I can't tell you how often I've heard this complaint.

If your subordinates don't understand precisely what

they're supposed to do, you can't have a non-dependent trust relationship with them. They're dependent by definition, trusting blindly that you'll look out for them and steer them in appropriate directions.

What could be more obvious? And yet why do so many managers and subordinates fail to agree on job responsibilities and expected results? Do you, for example, discuss the following when you introduce an assignment to a subordinate?

- Quantity

- Quality

- Costs

- Completion Date

- Communication Schedule

- Goals/Objectives

- Performance Evaluation

It's a short list, but how often do managers and subordinates discuss each point as they plan a project? When they do not, not only are employees more likely to head in the wrong direction but, even if they proceed correctly, they are probably less likely to achieve the proper goals than if they had a hand in establishing goals and setting directions. In general, employees are most productive if their objectives are:

- Set by the individual and the manager within the context of the division's objectives.

- Related to a specific task.

- Discussed in advance with an understanding of how and when they will be reviewed.

- Used as a basis for rewards.

- Discussed with others, if a group is involved, so that there is shared understanding of group objectives as well as of each individual's objectives.

A clear understanding of how the subordinate will be judged on his or her efforts is also fundamental to establishing a non-dependent trust relationship. Here are some basic do's and don'ts:

Do	*Don't*
Evaluate on the basis of accomplishment of objectives.	Evaluate on personality traits or image.
Give feedback regularly and close to the act.	Give an annual review only.
Evaluate work as it is accomplished.	Give an annual review only.
Measure quality as well as quantity.	Measure quantity only.
Measure individuals within their realistic potential.	Judge one employee against others with different skills and abilities.
Evaluate frequently.	Save up information about weaknesses.

(4) Don't Make Promises You Can't Keep

Living up to the policies outlined above isn't always easy. "Real world" conditions are often less than ideal for pursuing corporate philosophy. Take the line in the Johnson & Johnson credo that says employees "must have a sense of security in their jobs."

What happens during an economic downturn? What if offshore competition makes J&J employment costs substantially higher than those of its competitors? How does the company react to the marketplace without abandoning its corporate philosophy?

Obviously, creating a policy and then disregarding it is no better (and perhaps much worse) than having no philosophy in the first place. Management is wise to make no promises it cannot keep.

7

CREATING THE TRUST ENVIRONMENT

In the relationship between a manager and a subordinate, one of the most critical aspects of non-dependent
trust is a mutual sense of openness, the belief that each
individual can be trusted to speak his or her mind openly,
knowing that the other will listen with a helpful ear.

In such a trusting environment, subordinates feel free
to speak their minds, knowing that they'll at least get their
"day in court." They may not get their way, but they will
be heard. When individuals realize that they can speak up
and be listened to, they are more likely to follow management's lead, whatever direction it may take. The more
direct and open the communication, the better. In fact,
the manager's role in creating and nurturing a trust-based
relationship involves reacting in a positive, supportive
manner even when subordinates disagree or challenge.
This may not be easy in real life.

If the lines of open communication are established, the
subordinate sees the manager as a helper, or even a men-
tor, not as a judge. The manager sees the subordinate as
someone who is competent, involved, and willing to produce—and produce not just good work, but a trust environment as well.

Both are aware of their own, and the other's, responsibilities. The manager's responsibilities may include:

- Communicating directions clearly.

- Delegating tasks and responsibility.

- Permitting freedom and latitude in work
  methods.

- Encouraging risk-taking by subordinates.

- Treating failures as "lessons learned" that will avoid future mistakes.

- Making no unreasonable demands about objectives.

- Encouraging subordinates to request help.

- Permitting subordinates to question and disagree.

- Encouraging discussion of disagreements.

The subordinate's responsibilities may include:

- Reviewing directions and asking questions if the directions aren't clear.

- Accepting new responsibilities quickly.

- Thinking tasks through before beginning them.

- Asking superiors for guidance when necessary.

- Taking risks.

- Making decisions.

- Accepting—and even asking for—constructive criticism.

- Admitting mistakes and bringing them to the attention of management.

- Learning from mistakes.

- Raising questions, disagreeing, talking out problems.

- Recognizing the manager's responsibility to make final decisions.

- Following through on those decisions.

What can you as a manager do to improve your trust relationship with a subordinate? One priority should be to create an environment in which trust can flourish. One tactic for accomplishing this involves spending some time together away from the office.

Begin such a session by developing a list of things you and your subordinate share. Where do your attitudes and philosophy agree? What do you both want for your company or department?

You don't need to discover earth-shattering areas of agreement to start the process. I recall a speech I gave in Tokyo not long ago. I simply wasn't getting through to my audience of Japanese businessmen, who didn't crack a smile at any of my jokes. (I really couldn't blame them. I'm not the world's most accomplished storyteller.) At a reception following the speech, however, these formerly unsmiling individuals found that they could joke with me about my height (I'm 6'5"). All of a sudden, with one simple topic to share, we were laughing together and actually communicating with one another. Their polite but unresponsive looks disappeared for good.

Once you've found common ground with your subordinate, you can move ahead to two or three items on which you disagree. Discuss ways in which they might be resolved or minimized. Keep your discussions task-related. Instead of telling the subordinate, "You don't do this properly," ask, "Why do you think you and I approach the situation so differently?"

One of the most sensitive—and most important—times for building trust with subordinates is during performance reviews. The situation offers opportunities to cement relations or to destroy them.

Everyone is nervous at review time. Managers are ill at ease, because they almost always have some negative news to deliver. Subordinates worry that their reviews won't go well at all. The employee and his or her superior may start the session with points of view that are 180 degrees apart.

As a manager, you can use the review session to help your employees grow in their jobs, to make sure that they leave the session with an improved understanding of what is expected of them and how they can achieve their objectives. Even if you are dealing with an individual whose performance is inadequate, you can use the review opportunity to offer ways for improvement by giving supportive suggestions about performance.

Totally negative reviews most often fall on deaf ears. Most people simply can't handle a stream of negative feedback without getting more and more defensive. When we get defensive, we stop listening as we create our own arguments. When we stop listening, we stop learning.

Good reviews demand preparation. Before starting an evaluation, you might think about the following statements to establish a frame of mind that will be conducive to an effective performance review.

- No one is perfect.

- I'm not perfect.

- Managers aren't infallible.

- I'm going to evaluate this individual on work, not on personality.

- This review can help me work with my subordinate.

- This process can help me improve as a manager.

- I want this person to . . .

- We agree about . . .

- We disagree about . . .

- If there are things I don't like about this person, are they task-related or personal dislikes?

If you find that you're full of negative feelings as you're about to start a review, stop to collect your thoughts, or even postpone the meeting. Make sure you're not dumping your own problems onto your employee's shoulders. Needless to say, such actions won't improve the trust relationship.

It's not your job as a manager to be judge and jury in the review environment. A more effective role is that of a guide who directs the employee through a self-evaluation based on mutually agreed-upon objectives.

Here are some phrases to avoid:

- "I know you'll find this surprising . . ."

- "You probably didn't realize that you . . ."

If phrases like these are true, you probably haven't been doing your job as a manager. No real surprises should be introduced at review time, because performance issues should be identified and discussed as they surface in the day-to-day work environment. In addition, when you introduce such statements, your subordinate's immediate reaction is likely to be defensive. The employee shuts him- or herself out of the process, and it never really gets under way.

It's much more effective to adopt an interviewer's role and ask open-ended questions:

- How did this work?

- What problems did you have with that?

- How would you evaluate that?

- What could you have done to improve that?

When you take this approach, you begin to create a shared experience with your subordinate. The process helps both of you understand the present situation and look for ways to improve it.

Determining compensation and raises is another area in which a trust environment can be created or limited. At most American companies today, the system of allocating raises encourages distrust, because no one really understands just how compensation levels are determined.

Some companies have tried to address this issue by setting fixed raise guidelines, by which anyone receiving a rating of satisfactory or better gets the same percentage increase. One problem with this approach is that managers quickly learn that they must give their subordinates acceptable ratings if their employees are to receive any increase at all.

When mediocre and good performers get similar raises under such a program, the message comes through loud and clear: Why bother?

Most of us desperately want to believe that "the system" works, that it rewards individual effort, initiative, and achievement. Shatter this belief, and we begin to feel like cogs in a not-so-intelligent machine. In such an atmosphere, employees are likely to use their frustrated initiative to find ways of how to get by on less work, how not to worry about exceeding a budget, why it's OK to bring home an attaché case full of office supplies. If it's obvious that the company cares so little about you that it can't even figure out that you're doing your job better than that idiot down the hall, why care about the company?

Many corporations are trying to combat this problem by installing performance-based compensation systems. But here, too, compensation can only be equitable if the performance appraisal system is fair and accurate.

Group activities offer another way to nurture a trust environment in the workplace. When you bring people together to share ideas and attack problems as a team, you create a setting in which they can begin to trust themselves, each other, and you.

The group can discuss common problems that hinder the overall effectiveness of the organization or that damage individual effectiveness on the job. The group can work to set objectives and agree on shared expectations. Group members may begin to develop an informal leadership structure, as individuals who are particularly adept in certain areas are given daily responsibility for them. Often, as a result, the manager discovers less and less to worry about concerning day-to-day problems of running the business.

Group activities promote shared learning. In one-to-one meetings, subordinates might not question their bosses for fear of appearing unknowledgeable or stupid (even if it's the boss who isn't making sense). But in a group of their peers, they are much more likely to ask questions and challenge statements that don't ring true. When an individual really doesn't understand something, there is a group of people to choose from in search of clarification. If the entire group doesn't understand what the superior is looking for or talking about, its members can ask for more information as a group. No one person is singled out.

On an individual level, managers can work to create a trust environment by identifying and pursuing a range of goals that can be summarized in a series of statements:

- I work with subordinates to establish mutually agreed-upon objectives, goals and strategies for getting the job done.

- I allow subordinates to structure their work in ways that are comfortable and productive for them.

- I allow subordinates to make mistakes.

- I help my employees learn from mistakes in a supportive, non-judgmental manner.

- I encourage subordinates to say what they really think.

- I support group activity and peer counseling for problem solving and generation of ideas.

- I evaluate subordinates as individuals.

- As best I can within the corporate structure, I seek to compensate individuals for their efforts, and I discourage across-the-board salary increases.

- When I hire an employee, I explain the review process and work to build a trusting relationship.

- I have frequent, informal discussions with subordinates to discuss their work and progress.

- My subordinates know that there will be no unpleasant surprises during annual reviews.

8

THE LANGUAGE
OF TRUST

HOW WE ACT AND WHAT WE SAY obviously affect the way other people feel about us. Our words and actions can build trust, or we can act and speak in ways that inhibit, or even prevent, trust from developing.

Non-verbal trust language can be an important measure of how effectively we trust and how well we are trusted. The way we dress, how we decorate our offices, the messages our mannerisms send to others, even the way we sit—all demonstrate non-verbal trust language in action.

For instance, does your desk face the door or a window? Orienting your workspace toward its entrance suggests that you look forward to seeing people. Aim your desk out the window and, figuratively at least, you're turning your back on visitors.

When someone enters your office to speak with you, do you sit behind your desk, or do you arrange yourself and your guest so there are no barriers between you?

Your clothes can affect the way people feel about you. Studies indicate that people who dress in warm colors—reds, browns, and golds—tend to be trusted more readily than those who wear cool colors—blues, whites, and grays. (At the same time, if your company's culture suggests that successful people wear gray pinstripes, and you dress in brown plaids, your colleagues may not trust you.)

Your general bearing also sends messages that people interpret in terms of trustworthiness. Come across as stern, stiff, and judgmental, or as overly laid-back and non-responsive, or as exceptionally analytical, and others might not trust you intuitively. Come across as too outgoing and gregarious, and you might see the same result.

None of this may have anything whatsoever to do with whether you actually deserve to be trusted, of course. To be a successful con man, for example, you have to appear trustworthy. But if you are genuinely attempting to create and nurture a sense of trust on the job, it can prove valuable to examine not just what you do, but how you act and appear as well.

It's obvious, for instance, that you don't get people to trust you by playing power games: seating a visitor in a chair that's lower than yours, or positioning a guest so that he or she must look into a bright window, or ignoring people for a minute or so after they enter your office. Such gambits lock people into defensive behavior patterns that make building non-dependent trust virtually impossible.

Various theories have been advanced that it's a good idea to use such methods to manipulate subordinates or suppliers in order to gain "the upper hand." There are a couple of problems with this approach, however. First, your opponent—and by acting this way, you are surely creating an opponent—is likely to be thinking, "OK, you've got the advantage today, but I have a long memory, and I'll find a way to return the favor." Much more fundamental is the fact that it's just this sort of behavior that generates the kind of non-trusting, suspicious environment that causes so many problems in the first place. You don't just create mistrust in the one individual you manipulate; you create a work setting in which smart, sensitive employees know that it's dangerous to trust anyone. And the cycle continues.

Obviously, what you say and how you say it play a dominant role in whether you're perceived as a trustworthy individual. Business—and management in particular—is primarily a process of communication. And while most of us assume that our mouths are pretty closely connected to our brains, that what we say is a reasonable facsimile of what we're trying to say, this isn't necessarily the case. Most managers can tell stories about how they've given subordinates "simple, clear, and direct" instructions, only to receive work that bears absolutely no resemblance to what they wanted. Ultimately the work gets done, through a process of trial and error. The boss refines his or her instructions, and the subordinate hears and understands more clearly.

Or do they? The job might be completed at the expense of the trust relationship. Through words or actions, the boss makes it clear that if the employee was a little smarter, or showed a little more determination, or listened more attentively, the work could have been done correctly the first time around. After all, the boss gave clear directions for a relatively simple assignment, right?

In the meantime, the subordinate devotes half his energy to trying to figure out what on earth the boss really wants, and spends the other half developing an interior monologue that goes something like this: "This guy would have trouble explaining how to open a door, and on top of that, he never really *does* know what he wants. He never quite says it, but his message is very clear: it's always my fault when something goes wrong. I wonder what he tells *his* boss about me."

Language is powerful, and it can be used for positive or negative purposes. Used supportively, it can help people who are floundering to get back on track. Used negatively, it can undermine individuals and make trust relationships impossible. And, as the song says, "It ain't what you say, it's the way that you say it."

Each of us has a recognizable, habitual communication style. Typically, we communicate most easily and most effectively with people whose style is similar to our own. In fact, we can have real trouble communicating with individuals whose style differs from ours. Take an individual who thinks and communicates very precisely and systematically. "First do this, and when you're finished do that, and then report back to me with the results," he might instruct a subordinate.

Which is fine, unless the subordinate has a radically different communication style. "What's the real meaning behind this?" he might ask. "How does it relate to our overall goals and objectives?"

Unless the first individual is sensitive to this different, but equally valid, communication style, trouble can result. Tell the subordinate, "Look, I don't have time to sit here and chat about philosophy. Just do it, OK?" and the trust relationship is endangered. Spend a few minutes putting the assignment in perspective for the employee, so that it makes sense for him or her, and not only does the job get done, but the trust relationship between boss and employee is reinforced, just because the superior has taken the time to speak his subordinate's language.

There are four basic styles of communicator: Intuitor, Thinker, Feeler, and Senser. Which type are you? Answer the following questions to find out.

Communication Style Test

Indicate below the order in which you feel each choice best describes you. In the space provided, fill in the appropriate number using 1 for the answer that best fits you, 2 for the next one, 3 for the next, and 4 for the answer that is least appropriate for you.

1. I am likely to impress others as:
   a. practical and to the point   a. _____
   b. emotional and somewhat stimulating   b. _____
   c. astute and logical   c. _____
   d. intellectually oriented and somewhat complex   d. _____

2. When I work on a project, I:
   a. want it to be stimulating and involve lively interaction with others   a. _____
   b. concentrate to make sure it is systematically or logically developed   b. _____
   c. want to be sure it has a tangible pay-out that will justify my time and energy on it   c. _____
   d. am most concerned about whether it breaks ground or advances knowledge   d. _____

3. When I think about a job problem, I usually:
   a. think about concepts and relationships between events   a. _____

b. analyze what preceded it
and what I plan next   b. ____

c. remain open and
responsive to my feelings
about the matter   c. ____

d. concentrate on reality, on
things as they are right
now   d. ____

4. When confronted by others
with a different point of view, I
can usually make progress by:

a. getting at least one or two
specific commitments on
which we can build later   a. ____

b. trying to place myself in
the others' shoes   b. ____

c. keeping my composure
and helping others to see
things simply and logically   c. ____

d. relying on my basiç ability
to conceptualize and pull
ideas together   d. ____

5. In communicating with others,
I might:

a. express unintended
boredom with talk that is
too detailed   a. ____

b. convey impatience with
those who express ideas
that they have obviously
not thought through
carefully   b. ____

c. show little interest in thoughts and ideas that exhibit little or no originality   c. ____

d. tend to ignore those who talk about long-range implications and direct my attention to what needs to be done right now   d. ____

Analysis of Answers

To obtain an approximate indication of your primary communication style, enter below the number you wrote for each answer:

	Intuitor	Thinker	Feeler	Senser
Question 1	d. ____	c. ____	b. ____	a. ____
Question 2	d. ____	b. ____	a. ____	c. ____
Question 3	a. ____	b. ____	c. ____	d. ____
Question 4	d. ____	c. ____	b. ____	a. ____
Question 5	c. ____	b. ____	a. ____	d. ____
Totals	____	____	____	____

Total each column. The column that has the smallest sum indicates your favored communication style; the column with the largest total is your least-used style.

Intuitors look forward to the future with a global perspective. They are good with concepts and often are able to relate diverse thoughts and ideas into meaningful wholes. Most Intuitors display good innovative ability and skill at looking at "the big picture." Most planners are Intuitors.

Thinkers are people who desire to relate to their environment by thinking things through. As a result, Thinkers usually develop good analytical skills. Since facts and data are the tools with which one thinks, most Thinkers focus on being precise and systematic in their approach to problems. Many accountants are Thinkers. While the Intuitor's time orientation is in the future, the Thinker typically focuses on the entire spectrum. Thinkers want to know about the factors that lead up to a particular situation (historical background), what is happening now, and what the outcome will be.

Feelers prefer to deal with situations according to their "feeling" perceptions; that is, they frequently respond with gut reactions. Feelers are highly sociable and use empathy and understanding in their solutions to problems. Most of them are perceptive of others' needs and are able to discern what lies beneath the surface. Their time orientation is essentially toward the past. Many sales persons are Feelers.

Sensers are here-and-now oriented. As a result, most Sensers respond to things they can touch, see, and feel—things of an immediate nature. They tend to be action oriented and are often found in production and high-pressure job situations.

No communication style is "good" or "bad." Any style can be used effectively, just as any can be taken to excess. The important thing is to recognize that different people have different styles and to be sensitive to these differences.

If individuals need to be sensitive about communications on the job, companies do, too. Not all companies communicate successfully, however. When business is good, for example, many firms don't do much to celebrate. When business is bad, many organizations try to obscure the situation rather than communicate it.

When things go wrong, it's rare for a company to admit, "We blew it last year, and the competition beat us." It's much more likely that statements like these will be made: "We're going to concentrate on getting lean and mean." "It's back to basics for the company." "It's time to focus on shirtsleeve management." Such language typically translates to "Business is down, we're going to fire some people, and anyone who's left ought to feel grateful working three times harder than they are today."

Why not just say, "Business is off and we're going to have to let some people go"? For one thing, many companies worry that if they admit problems, their best people—the individuals they desperately need to retain if they are to turn the situation around—will jump ship. Only the sick, the lame, and the infirm will remain, and the situation will continue to deteriorate.

In fact, while it's true that some valuable employees may leave, most people will stay on the job until the bitter end. They may enjoy their work, or may be loyal to the company, or may simply fear the search for a new job.

When we counsel companies that face a downsizing we advise management to inform employees about conditions as quickly as possible. There are then no major surprises if layoffs do prove necessary, and the people who remain with the company have better feelings about the organization than if they had to witness a Friday-afternoon massacre.

Some companies can't be trusted even when business is good. Hoping to generate additional profits, some managements adopt a perpetual hangdog posture: "Business isn't too good," they say; "the wolf is at the door." They publicize industry problems, focus on any slight downturn in the economy, all in an attempt to keep employee expectations down.

I knew one advertising agency chairman who was a master at this game. He seemed to have a sixth sense about when his employees were poised to ask for raises. Just when it seemed obvious that the agency was making money hand over fist, he would send out a memo saying that the next quarter's projections looked a little weak, and that he hoped no one would have to be laid off. Before too long, his most able employees began to feel abused and, what may have been worse, decided that they were being treated like idiots. They began to leave the agency, which certainly did keep raises down, but which had even greater negative impact on profits.

We've talked about other kinds of communication that destroy trust—for example, the type of paternalistic language that some managers use to instill loyalty or to avoid difficult situations: "Don't worry, I'll take care of you," or "You'll always have a job here at ACME," or "You look out for me, and I'll look out for you."

If you ever use such phrases, consider them carefully before you repeat them again. Do you have the power to follow through on them? Even if you own the company, can you guarantee your employees that they'll always have a future there? The first time you fail to deliver on a promise, your trust relationship with employees begins to erode. Watch your trust language.

9

WHAT'S <u>YOUR</u> TRUST LEVEL?

I BELIEVE that the most practical way to improve trust in the workplace is to begin close to home: with ourselves. To do that, we need to examine our own trust levels. How much—or how little—do we really trust our superiors, our subordinates, and our company? How much do the people we work for trust us? What about the individuals who work for us?

As I began to work on this book, I realized that there was no easy way to assess levels of trust. We can't measure it in pounds or pints, and while we can say, "I don't trust him at all," or "I'd trust her with my life," trying to articulate feelings that lie between these extremes gets to be a murky process.

So it seemed that developing a method to measure or assess trust might provide a useful management tool. The short surveys that follow are based on lengthier instruments developed with the assistance of Dr. Elaine Duffy, a psychologist. The materials were later reviewed by The Psychological Corporation.

Four surveys are included here, two for subordinates and two for managers. Since virtually everyone assumes both roles in his or her business life, we suggest that you complete all four instruments. We've also found that these materials are most useful when an individual's boss and subordinates also complete them.

To date, hundreds of individuals representing virtually every imaginable boss-subordinate relationship have used these surveys to sharpen their focus on important trust issues. In addition, we've used the instruments in a Drake Beam Morin training program that addresses the issue of performance evaluations and seeks to shape that process as a shared experience between manager and employee. In essence, we try to show that whenever managers evaluate a subordinate's activities, they are also evaluating their own performance.

These materials have proven very useful in both settings, but it's important to note that the surveys are not validated psychological instruments. They're learning tools that can help you and your boss or subordinate structure a dialogue about trust relationships.

The "right" answers to the statements in these surveys are obvious. But if you approach this exercise like a test and try to earn an A+ by filling in "correct" responses, you'll waste your time. The key is to be as honest as you can about your sense of trust on the job. Parenthetically, if you find it difficult to be honest about your superiors, or if one of your subordinates agrees to complete the surveys but gives answers about you that sound too good to be true, you may already have learned an important lesson about trust in your organization.

Trust Surveys

Each of the four surveys presents you with a series of descriptive statements.

If you **Strongly Agree** with the statement, write the number 4 in the box following it.

If you **Agree** with the statement, write the number 3.

If you **Disagree** with the statement, write the number 2.

If you **Strongly Disagree** with the statement, write the number 1.

Once you've entered responses for all the statements in the survey, add up your total. The evaluations that follow each survey compare your score to that of people in positions similar to yours who have previously responded to the survey.

Repeat this process for each of the four surveys.

Each survey has been developed as part of a project that involved hundreds of people from all management levels and from many different departments and types of organizations. Keep in mind, however, that they are only samples of longer questionnaires developed for use in large-scale projects. As such, they offer insight into general feelings, not exact measurements of trust levels.

Survey 1

Managers Trusting Subordinates

1. I make it a point to follow through on my promises. ☐

2. I delegate projects that enable my subordinates to attain success. ☐

3. I delegate as much work as possible without abdicating my own responsibilities. ☐

4. Each of my subordinates has the knowledge and skills required for his or her job. ☐

5. My subordinates believe that I have the knowledge and skills required for my job. ☐

6. My subordinates understand my style of management. ☐

7. My subordinates feel confident that the information I give them is accurate. ☐

8. My subordinates are aware that I take their opinions and suggestions seriously. ☐

9. I involve my subordinates in important decisions concerning the individual or the department. ☐

10. I can be relied on to handle work-related situations with good judgment. ☐

Total Score: _____

Evaluation: Survey 1
Managers Trusting Subordinates

If your score falls between:

10–20   Your Trust Quotient on this factor is low. You have real concerns about the quality of your communications with your subordinates, and you question the level of trust that exists in these relationships.

21–25   Your Trust Quotient on this factor is a little below average. You are concerned about your ability to trust your working relationships with some of your subordinates, and you may feel a need to improve your capability to work toward common goals.

26–34   Your Trust Quotient on this factor is somewhat above average. You feel that you have adequate working relationships with your subordinates, and you believe you can function well as a team.

35–40   Your Trust Quotient on this factor is at its highest level. You have a strong trust relationship with your subordinates, you feel that you communicate well with them, and you are confident that your team works together cohesively.

Survey 2

Managers Trusting Top Management

1. My view of compensation is consistent with the organization's compensation policies. ☐

2. The organization supports the way I approach my subordinates. ☐

3. My subordinates understand my influence within the decision-making hierarchy of the organization. ☐

4. Top management creates an environment in which people motivate and direct themselves toward a common goal. ☐

5. My subordinates are rewarded for independent thought. ☐

6. My manager communicates an interest in my career. ☐

7. Top management has the best interests of its employees in mind. ☐

8. My suggestions and ideas are heard by top management. ☐

9. My organization has clearly defined its corporate goals and business objectives. ☐

10. Top management shares information about its business philosophy. ☐

Total Score: _____

Evaluation: Survey 2
Managers Trusting Top Management

If your score falls between:

10–20   Your Trust Quotient on this factor is low. You feel isolated from top management, you don't believe that your views (or those of your subordinates) are supported, and your general level of trust in this area is questionable.

21–25   Your Trust Quotient on this factor is a little below average. You feel somewhat removed from top management and would like to feel that your views, and the views of your staff, were supported more consistently.

26–34   Your Trust Quotient on this factor is somewhat above average. You believe that there is adequate communication with top management, and that opportunities are available to gain some support for your views and those of your team.

35–40   Your Trust Quotient on this factor is very high. You feel that both you and your subordinates are supported by top management, and that lines of communication are open. A healthy level of agreement appears to exist between your areas of responsibility and those of your top management.

Survey 3

Subordinates Trusting Managers

1. My manager communicates that he or she respects my skills and abilities. ☐

2. My manager encourages me to take risks and make decisions. ☐

3. My manager always informs me about important matters that affect me. ☐

4. I feel free to tell my manager what's on my mind. ☐

5. My manager encourages me to develop and grow professionally. ☐

6. My manager has the skills and knowledge required for his or her job. ☐

7. My manager encourages me to determine my own objectives. ☐

8. I'm comfortable sharing personal thoughts or inner feelings with my manager. ☐

9. My efforts to demonstrate initiative are openly appreciated by my manager. ☐

10. My manager involves me in important decisions concerning me or my department. ☐

Total Score: _____

Evaluation: Survey 3
Subordinates Trusting Managers

If your score falls between:

10–20   Your Trust Quotient on this factor is at the lowest level. You feel your supervisor does not offer you much support, and you do not communicate openly and effectively with your manager.

21–25   Your Trust Quotient on this factor is a little below average. You would like to see some improvement in the level of trust that exists in your interactions with your boss, and you think that he or she needs to be more consistent in providing an environment of openness and support.

26–34   Your Trust Quotient on this factor is somewhat above average. You approve of the way you communicate with your boss, and you tend to feel comfortable with the general exchange of information and ideas between you and your manager.

35–40   Your Trust Quotient on this factor is at the highest level. You believe that you have an open and effective working relationship with your boss, and you believe that he or she has a real interest in your potential and your ideas.

Survey 4

Subordinates Trusting Top Management

1. The organization supports my manager's approach with his or her staff. ☐

2. My manager is loyal to me and to the department. ☐

3. I tend to be honest and truthful in my communications with my manager. ☐

4. Top management allocates resources to support innovation. ☐

5. The company supports my manager's performance appraisal policies. ☐

6. When necessary, I willingly submit to management's directives. ☐

7. My manager gives me frequent "pats on the back." ☐

8. The negative feedback I receive from my manager is helpful and constructive. ☐

9. My ideas and suggestions are heard by top management. ☐

10. My manager spends adequate time communicating with top management. ☐

Total Score: _____

Evaluation: Survey 4
Subordinates Trusting Top Management

If your score falls between:

10–20   Your Trust Quotient on this factor is at the lowest level. You feel isolated from top management and do not believe that your opinion and input are considered to be important. Your confidence in the directions of top management is questionable.

21–25   Your Trust Quotient on this factor is a little below average. You feel somewhat removed from top management and may be uncertain about the organization's ability to hear your ideas or those of your manager.

26–34   Your Trust Quotient on this factor is a little above average. You believe that there is an open line of communication with top management and that your skills and abilities, as well as those of your manager, are appreciated adequately.

35–40   Your Trust Quotient on this factor is at the highest level. You feel supported by top management and trust that you are recognized as a contributor to the organization.

The results of these surveys can be used by individuals—or by entire companies—as tools to gain clarity about how trust relationships can be improved. As an individual, your answers and scores can tell you a great deal about your attitudes regarding trust at your company. Combine and compare the results of all the individuals in a department—or in an entire company—and you've gained a "big-picture" view of trust attitudes within the organization.

These results might be used, in turn, in the design of training programs, communication skills workshops, or performance appraisal systems, all focused on the goal of getting the very best possible from the company's principal resource: its people.

AFTERWORD

As OUR WORLD CHANGES, our notion of trust changes with it—and not always for the better. Trust seems to be under attack today, not just in business but throughout society.

The "Me" mentality that characterized the yuppie phenomenon of the eighties was a recent (and certainly a well-publicized) example of this erosion in trust. The notion of a class of young people earning substantial (many would say excessive) incomes, and apparently having no goals beyond earning substantially more, became etched in the public consciousness. Here was a group that appeared to trust nothing beyond fancy cars and high living.

Characterizations like this are obviously the product of generalization and stereotyping. But just as certainly, there was something going on here. The general scorn directed at the whole notion of yuppiedom suggests that society in general wants something more from its business community than just the bottom line.

In the middle of 1987, I recall talking with a group of young investment bankers. I suspect each would have denied it, but I knew I'd entered a den of yuppies. I came away from the discussion with one overriding and unsettling memory.

To a man—and woman—this group of bright, well-educated, energetic people insisted that the companies that employed them had no interest in them beyond their capacity to generate fees and commissions. Falter in that objective, they felt, and they would be dumped unceremoniously. They were resources to be consumed.

There was no sense of trust in their work environment on the part of these young people, a situation caused, I think, by a lack of real trust on the part of their employers.

What kind of trust might both have pursued? Not the blind "We'll take care of you" variety, certainly. The October 1987 stock market crash (in whose wake the label "yuppie" became academic for so many people who lost jobs) showed just how impossible it is to support that definition of trust. You simply can't take a market trading 240 million shares a day, turn it overnight into a market trading 120 million shares, and tell people, "We'll take care of you." People are going to be hurt.

But I can't believe that the solution to this dilemma is to take the humanity out of the workplace and say in effect, "We don't—or we can't—care about you, we only care about what you produce. You're one more machine in this factory."

What I've tried to lay out in this book is another way, one that accounts for both the needs of the marketplace and our needs as humans. It's a way that admits that life can be dangerous by saying, "If you don't produce, or if the rest of us don't produce, or if the stock market crashes, or perhaps even if someone crashes an oil tanker into an Alaskan reef, you may be out of a job."

But it's also a way that promotes a sense of community by announcing, "You're part—an important part—of this organization. Ultimately, you're responsible to and for yourself, but you're part of this group, too. We'll train you, listen to you, value and reward your contributions, tell you how you're doing, and tell you how we're doing. We'll be open and aboveboard with you, and we expect the same in return."

There is nothing new in all this, no unique discoveries or scientific breakthroughs. But it comes at a time when our society seems to be afflicted with symptoms of disintegration: homelessness and single-parent families, record school dropout statistics, and terrifying crime rates. It all suggests that many of our institutions are imperiled.

At a time when we can't seem to keep the oil off the beaches or the acid rain out of the lakes, we also seem unable to manage our businesses or our human resources. I worry that time is running out. I believe now is the time to put real—and caring—life back into the workplace. It simply will not work without that very human trait called non-dependent trust.